Union Public Library

MACHINES ★ AT WORK

MOTORCYCLES

BY CYNTHIA ROBERTS

THE CHILD'S WORLD® • MANKATO, MINNESOTA

The Child's World®

Published in the United States of America by The Child's World®
1980 Lookout Drive • Mankato, MN 56003-1705
800-599-READ • www.childsworld.com

PHOTO CREDITS
© David M. Budd Photography: 12, 16
© iStockphoto.com/Andrea Leone: 4
© iStockphoto.com/Christine Balderas: 3
© iStockphoto.com/Damir Spanic: cover, 2
© iStockphoto.com/Jan Tyler: 19
© iStockphoto.com/Jason Turcotte: 7
© iStockphoto.com/Joe Richter: 20
© iStockphoto.com/Justin Allfree: 15
© iStockphoto.com/Ralf Hirsch: 8
© iStockphoto.com/Shaun Lowe: 11

9/08

ACKNOWLEDGMENTS
The Child's World®: Mary Berendes, Publishing Director;
Katherine Stevenson, Editor

The Design Lab: Kathleen Petelinsek, Design and Page Production

LIBRARY OF CONGRESS CATALOGING-IN-PUBLICATION DATA
Roberts, Cynthia, 1960–
   Motorcycles / by Cynthia Roberts.
      p. cm. — (Machines at work)
   Includes bibliographical references and index.
   ISBN 1-59296-833-3 (library bound : alk. paper)
   1. Motorcycles—Juvenile literature. I. Title. II. Series.
   TL440.15.R633 2007
   629.227'5—dc22   2006023298

 Contents

Sport bikes can go fast! A helmet and special clothes help keep this rider safe.

What are motorcycles?

Motorcycles are **vehicles** with only two wheels. They are like big, heavy bicycles. Bicycles have foot pedals to make them go. Motorcycles have a powerful **engine** instead. Motorcycles can go much faster than bicycles!

What are the parts of a motorcycle?

A motorcycle has **handlebars** above the front wheel. It has a seat for the driver. The engine is under the seat. Most motorcycle engines burn gasoline to make power. The power is used to turn the back wheel. That makes the motorcycle move.

handlebars

seat

engine

This motorcycle's handlebars have several controls.

How do you drive a motorcycle?

To drive a motorcycle, you use both hands and both feet. There are **controls** on the handlebars. There are more controls near your feet. Some controls make the motorcycle go faster or slower. Others make the motorcycle stop.

9

At low speeds, you steer a motorcycle like a bicycle. You turn the handlebars to make the motorcycle turn. You do not have to turn the handlebars very far! At higher speeds, leaning to one side or the other helps you turn.

This rider is leaning to turn the motorcycle.

This police officer is watching other cars. He makes sure other drivers are safe. He can move his motorcycle quickly if something goes wrong.

How are motorcycles used for work?

Motorcycles are helpful for some kinds of jobs. Some police officers drive them. Police motorcycles have **sirens** and lights. They can move quickly. Sometimes they go where police cars cannot fit.

How are motorcycles used for fun?

Lots of people ride motorcycles for fun. Some people even race them! There are many kinds of motorcycle racing. Different types of racing use different types of motorcycles.

This racer is just about to cross the finish line. Crouching low helps the motorcycle go faster.

This rider is driving his dirt bike on sand. He must use his body to help turn the bike.

People also ride off-road motorcycles for fun. Dirt bikes are made for riding on bumpy dirt trails. They are good for jumping, too.

17

Some people ride motorcycles when they go on vacation. **Touring** motorcycles are easy to ride on long trips. They have extra space for carrying things. Some even pull trailers!

18

These people are riding their touring motorcycles in Vermont.

Some people have fun making their motorcycles look different!

Are motorcycles useful?

People all over the world ride
motorcycles. Motorcycles have lots
of different uses. They need less
gasoline than cars. They are fun
to ride, too. No wonder so many
people like them!

21

 # Glossary

controls (kun-TROHLZ) Controls are parts that people use to run a machine.

engine (EN-jun) An engine is a machine that makes something move.

handlebars (HAN-dul BARZ) Handlebars are the steering bars on a motorcycle or bicycle.

sirens (SY-runz) Sirens make loud noises to let people know there is danger.

touring (TUR-ing) Touring is taking a trip, often to sightsee.

vehicles (VEE-ih-kullz) Vehicles are things that carry people or goods.

 Books

Siebert, Diane, and Leonard Jenkins (illustrator). *Motorcycle Song*. New York: HarperCollins, 2002.

Stuart, Dee. *Motorcycles*. Berkeley Heights, NJ: Enslow Publishers, 2001.

 Web Sites

Visit our Web site for lots of links about motorcycles:
http://www.childsworld.com/links
Note to parents, teachers, and librarians: We routinely check our Web links to make sure they're safe, active sites—so encourage your readers to check them out!

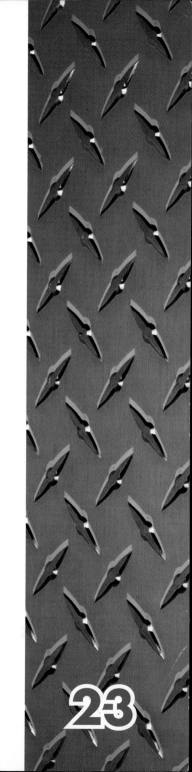

23

 # Index

 # About the Author

Even as a child, Cynthia Roberts knew she wanted to be a writer. She is always working to involve kids in reading and writing, and she loves spending time in the children's section of the library or bookstore. Cynthia enjoys gardening, traveling, and having fun with friends and family.